Build a Solar Cooker

BY SAMANTHA S. BELL · ILLUSTRATED BY ROGER STEWART

Published by The Child's World®
1980 Lookout Drive · Mankato, MN 56003-1705
800-599-READ · www.childsworld.com

Acknowledgments
The Child's World®: Mary Swensen, Publishing Director
Red Line Editorial: Editorial direction and production
The Design Lab: Design

Photographs © Byelikova Oksana/iStockphoto/Thinkstock, 5; Nina Lishchuk/Shutterstock Images, 6; David Franklin/Shutterstock Images, 8

Design Elements: JosephTodaro/Texturevault; Shutterstock Images

ISBN 9781503807884

LCCN 2015958135

Printed in the United States of America
Mankato, MN
June, 2016
PA02301

ABOUT THE AUTHOR

Samantha S. Bell is the author of more than 30 nonfiction books for children. She loves spending time in her yard in South Carolina. Her favorite days are those she spends outdoors making something new.

ABOUT THE ILLUSTRATOR

Roger Stewart has been an artist and illustrator for more than 30 years. His first job involved drawing aircraft parts. Since then, he has worked in advertising, design, film, and publishing. Roger has lived in London, England, and Sydney, Australia, but he now lives on the southern coast of England.

Contents

CHAPTER ONE

Using the Sun

Have you ever helped cook a meal for your family? Maybe you put water in a pot to boil. Or you may have helped take vegetables out of an oven. Perhaps you flipped hamburgers on a grill or roasted hot dogs over a fire. If so, you know it takes a lot of heat to cook food.

Heat is made in many different ways. Some ovens use electricity to make heat. Others use **natural gas**. Burning **charcoal** and wood creates heat, too. But did you know you can cook with the heat from the sun?

Energy from the sun is called solar energy. Solar energy helps keep us warm outside. But it can also be used to cook food. Solar cooking is a safe and simple way to cook.

There are many types of solar cookers. All of them use the sun for heat. In a box cooker, sunlight shines through a clear window. Some of the light is taken in by dark surfaces inside the cooker. The light is changed to heat energy. The heat energy cannot go through the window. It is trapped in the box. **Insulation**

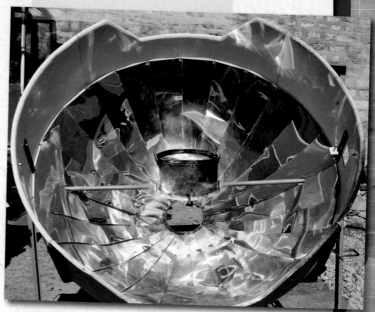

Parabolic solar cookers are curved. They cook foods at high temperatures.

helps keep it inside. The heat energy cooks the food. A box cooker can cook at medium to high temperatures.

Some people cook only with solar cookers. They do not use ovens at all. Some of their food takes a long time to cook. People may have trouble cooking difficult recipes with a solar cooker. Solar cookers cannot cook on cloudy days or at night. But they have many benefits.

CHAPTER TWO

Good for People

Solar cookers can be used to cook all types of foods. They cook without using extra water. When food is cooked with water, some of the nutrients are taken out. Solar cookers help keep the **nutrients** inside the food.

Many people cook over fires. Smoke from the fires can be harmful for people.

For many people, using a solar cooker is the safest way to cook food. Gas ovens make harmful gases, such as carbon monoxide. Carbon monoxide can make people feel sick or dizzy. In some countries, people do not have electricity or ovens. They must cook over fires in their homes. The fires create smoke.

People can become sick if they breathe in too much smoke. Solar cookers do not give off harmful gasses.

Solar cookers can also be used to **purify** water. This is especially important in countries that do not have clean water. Dirty water has germs in it. The germs can make people sick. Heating the water to 149 degrees Fahrenheit (65°C) kills the germs. The cooker makes the water safe to drink.

Solar cookers have other benefits. Unlike ovens, they are easy to move. They make cooking easier, too. You do not need to tend to food in a solar cooker as closely as with other types of cooking. The food does not need to be stirred.

Solar cookers can also help people with chores. People can heat water in a solar cooker to use to clean tables, chairs, and floors. Dishes can be washed and then set in the solar cooker. The heat makes the dishes germfree.

SOLAR SAVINGS

You probably use natural gas or electricity in your home. Your family pays for these energy sources. Cooking in an oven raises the cost. But the energy from the sun is free. Using a solar cooker is a good way to save money.

CHAPTER THREE

Good for Nature

Solar cookers are good for people. They are also good for Earth. A solar cooker uses sunlight. Sunlight is a renewable energy source. We will not run out of sunlight. Other energy sources are limited.

You can reuse a pizza box to make a solar cooker.

Most of our electricity comes from burning coal and natural gas. This makes carbon dioxide. Carbon dioxide is a greenhouse gas. Greenhouse gases trap heat. Having too much of these gases may make Earth warmer. Solar cookers do not use electricity. They do not give off any gases.

Many people around the world cook over fires every day. Burning wood also makes greenhouse gases. But there's another problem. Trees must be cut down for firewood. In some places, too many trees are cut. The forests are disappearing.

Some people buy solar cookers. Other people make their own. They can use materials they already have. Solar cookers can be made from cardboard or wood. Some people use glass from old windows. Other people use old newspapers and metal pieces. People help Earth by reusing materials instead of throwing them away.

You can build your own solar cooker. Then you can cook a snack in it. You will have a tasty treat. And you will be taking care of nature.

WORKING TOGETHER

In the 1970s, two friends made one of the first cardboard solar cookers. They showed people solar cookers could be useful, cheap, and safe. You too can make a difference with your friends. You can tell them about the benefits of using a solar cooker.

CHAPTER FOUR

Building a Solar Cooker

Solar cookers come in many shapes and sizes. Some can get very hot. These can cook food quickly. Others take longer to cook. A box cooker heats up slowly. But the food inside will not burn.

You can make your own box cooker. Be sure to build it on a sunny day. You may find many of the materials around your home. You might need to buy a few things at the store. The best part: before you begin, you will probably need to order a pizza. Let's get started!

WHICH WORKS BEST?

There are many ways to make a solar cooker. You don't have to use a pizza box. You could use a shoebox instead. Any cardboard box with a lid will work. You can also use a pie tin instead of a paper plate. Try different designs. See which one works the best for you.

MATERIALS

- ☐ Pizza box
- ☐ Pencil
- ☐ Ruler
- ☐ Scissors
- ☐ Aluminum foil
- ☐ Glue stick
- ☐ Black construction paper
- ☐ Plastic wrap
- ☐ Masking tape
- ☐ Newspaper
- ☐ Paper plate
- ☐ Thermometer

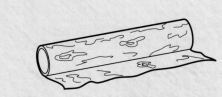

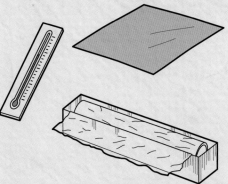

INSTRUCTIONS

STEP 1: Close the box's flap. Take the pencil. Draw a new flap onto the box's flap. Each side of the new flap should be at least 2 inches (5 cm) from the sides of the original flap. The new flap will attach to the box on the same side as the original flap.

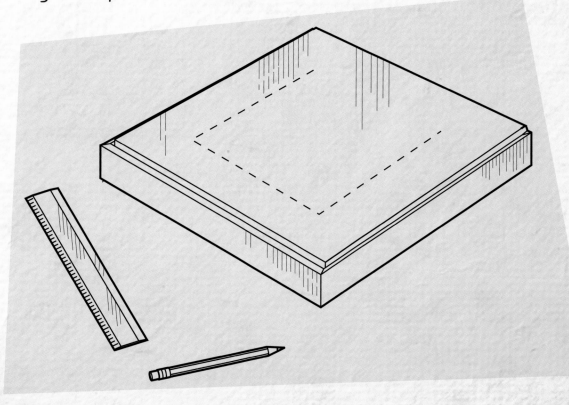

STEP 2: Take the scissors. Cut along the line you have drawn. Open the new flap. Fold it back.

STEP 3: Next, cut a piece of foil. Make it big enough to cover the bottom of the new flap.

STEP 4: One side of the foil will be shinier. Turn the foil so the shiny side faces toward you. Glue the foil to the bottom of the flap. It will **reflect** sunlight into the box.

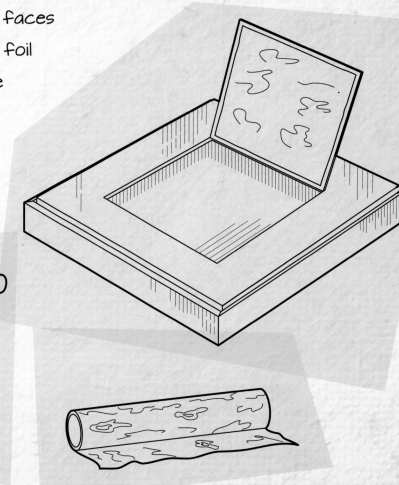

STEP 5: Open the box. Cut the black paper so it covers the floor of the box. Glue the paper down. The dark color will help the paper take in heat from the sunlight.

STEP 7: Measure the size of the opening you cut into the box. Cut a sheet of plastic wrap that is .5 inches (1.3 cm) wider and taller than the opening. Then, cut a second sheet to the same size.

STEP 8: Put the first piece of plastic over the opening on the top of the lid. Tape the plastic wrap in place.

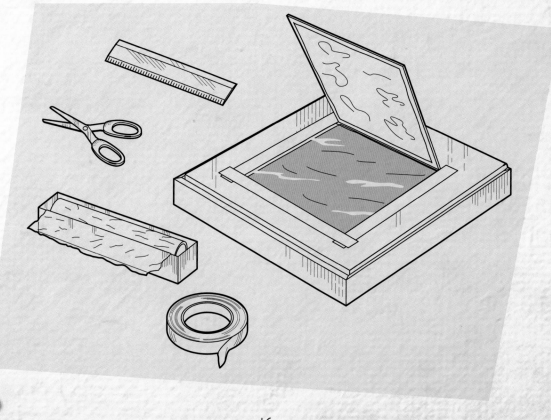

STEP 9: Open the box. Put the second piece of plastic over the opening on the bottom side. Tape the plastic in place. Now you have two layers of plastic over the opening. The plastic will let the sunlight into the box.

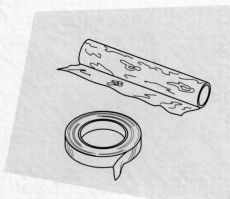

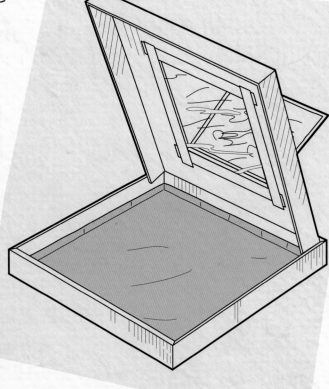

STEP 10: Open the box's lid. Roll up a sheet of newspaper. The roll should be about the height of the box and the length of one side. Put the roll of paper inside the box along one wall. Leave some space between the roll and the wall so the flap can close. Tape the roll to the bottom of the box. The newspaper will help keep heat in the box.

STEP 11: Add newspaper rolls to the other three sides of the box. Make sure the lid can close tightly.

STEP 12: Open the box. Place the paper plate on the black paper. Tape the thermometer to the floor of the box.

IS IT HOT IN HERE?

Check the thermometer at the same time every day. Record the temperatures in a journal or notebook. Be sure also to write down the weather for that day. Notice how the weather outside affects the temperature inside the cooker.

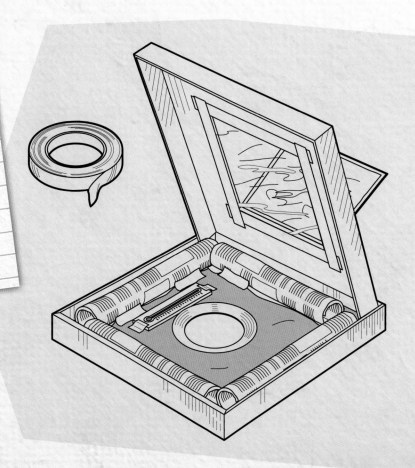

WHAT TO MAKE

S'mores are an easy snack to make with your cooker. First, warm up a marshmallow on top of a graham cracker in your cooker. Then, add chocolate on top and wait for it to melt.

You can also make a mini pizza. Spread pizza sauce on a piece of pita bread. Then, add toppings, such as cheese and pepperoni. Place it on a plate. Put the plate in the cooker. When the cheese melts, the pizza is done.

STEP 13: Place your solar cooker in the sunlight. Make sure nothing will get in between it and the sun's rays. Put the food you want to cook onto the plate. Carefully close the lid of the solar cooker.

STEP 14: Open the flap you have made. Prop it open with the ruler. The foil on the bottom of the flap will reflect the sunlight. Make sure the light is reflecting into the box. Once it is positioned correctly, tape the ruler in place. You are ready to cook.

As your food heats up, make sure to keep the sunlight reflecting into the box. You may need to adjust the ruler.

GLOSSARY

charcoal (CHAHR-kohl) Charcoal is a form of carbon found in wood or other substances. Many people burn charcoal when they cook on grills.

insulation (in-suh-LEY-shun) Insulation is material used to stop the transfer of heat. Insulation helps homes stay warm in the winter.

natural gas (NACH-er-uhl GAS) Natural gas is a gas that occurs underground and is used as fuel. Some ovens and heaters use natural gas.

nutrients (NOO-tree-uhnts) Nutrients are substances that help something grow. Fresh vegetables are full of nutrients.

purify (PYOOR-uh-fahy) To purify is to make clean. You must purify water from a river before you drink it.

reflect (ri-FLEKT) To reflect is to bend or throw back waves of light. Jewelry and other shiny objects reflect sunlight.

TO LEARN MORE

In the Library

Honovich, Nancy, and Julie Beer. *National Geographic Kids Get Outside Guide: All Things Adventure, Exploration, and Fun!* Washington, DC: National Geographic, 2014.

Leedy, Loreen. *The Shocking Truth about Energy*. New York: Holiday House, 2011.

Lewis, Rose. *Solar Energy*. Northampton, MA: Pioneer Valley, 2011.

Spetgang, Tilly. *The Kids' Solar Energy Book*. Bournemouth, UK: Imagine, 2011.

On the Web

Visit our Web site for links about solar cookers: **childsworld.com/links**

Note to Parents, Teachers, and Librarians:
We routinely verify our Web links to make sure
they are safe and active sites. So encourage
your readers to check them out!

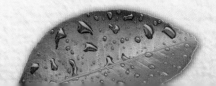

INDEX